woolley wood
Art

# Step by Step
# Display in the
# Primary School

**by Dianne Williams**

# Introduction

The preparation of good displays and exhibitions takes time and effort but the educational pay off can be enormous. This book aims to offer tips, ideas and suggestions to help in the preparation and layout of displays. It gives suggestions as to ways of making the most effective use of the space, time and resources available in order to achieve the maximum impact both within the classroom setting and in other parts of the school environment.

It includes illustrations of different approaches to display, step by step instructions on mounting, arranging and labelling displays and useful tools and materials to consider as part of a 'display kit'.

The book offers suggestions for creating displays that encourage thinking, research, investigation, involvement, questioning, interaction, appreciation and enjoyment, all of which contribute to and support teaching and learning both within the classroom and the school as a whole.

Ideas for storage of materials and equipment are also considered. Because space is at a premium in most rooms and a wealth of resources are constantly in use, the way materials and equipment are set out can detract from rather than enhance the appearance of the environment. Ideas for overcoming such problems are both illustrated and suggested.

Health and safety issues in relation to display are discussed as are the pitfalls best avoided and the points to aim for in order to achieve displays that improve the quality of the school environment. These hopefully in turn, influence the way the children feel about their classroom environment, the way they use it, learn from it and have care and consideration for it.

Finally my thanks to the teachers in the many schools that have helped in the production of this book by willingly contributing photographs of the stunning displays that have been part of their children's learning environment.

Dianne Williams

Schools which have provided work for this book include:

Ashton Primary School
Barrow Primary School
Broad Oak Primary School
Deepdale Infant School
Haslingden Primary School
Manor Beech Primary School
Moss Side Primary School
Whitefield Infants School
Woodplumpton C.E.Primary School
St Theresa's Primary School

Many other Lancashire schools have also offered inspiration for this work.

Step by Step Art Books are available from all good Educational Bookshops and by mail order from:

Topical Resources, P.O. Box 329, Broughton, Preston, Lancashire. PR3 5LT

Topical Resources publishes a range of Educational Materials for use in Primary Schools and Pre-School Nurseries and Playgroups.

For the latest catalogue:
**Tel 01772 863158**
**Fax 01772 866153**
e.mail: sales@topical-resources.co.uk
Visit our Website at: www.topical-resources.co.uk

Copyright © Dianne Williams

Printed in Great Britain for 'Topical Resources', Publishers of Educational Materials, P.O. Box 329, Broughton, Preston, Lancashire PR3 5LT by T.Snape & Company Limited, Boltons Court, Preston Lancashire.

Typeset by Paul Sealey Illustration & Design, 3 Wentworth Drive, Thornton, Lancashire.

First Published September 2003.

ISBN 1 872977 84 7

# Contents

# Displays and their Purpose

## Aims

Displays should aim to:
- Make the environment interesting and attractive.
- Communicate ideas and information clearly and simply.
- Show the process of work undertaken as well as the product.
- Stimulate interest and curiosity.
- Show appreciation of children's work.
- Respond to, enrich and extend the interests of the children.
- Reflect the general ethos of the school itself.

## Observe

Displays should aim to encourage children individually and collaboratively to observe:
- The environment outside the school i.e. the natural and man-made environment around them.
- The environment within the school grounds i.e. playground areas and gardens.
- The environmental spaces within school that are shared i.e. foyers, corridors and resource areas.
- The environment within the classroom i.e. objects, pictures, books and photographs selected to stimulate curiosity and interest related to current learning.

## Question

Displays should aim to encourage children to question:
- Why?
- What?
- How?
- Where?
- When?
- Who?
- To make comparisons and to look for similarities and differences.
- To express opinions.
- To evaluate and discuss their work and that of others.
- To gain ideas and to share ideas.
- To see, enjoy and appreciate the work of other year groups.

## Investigate

Displays should aim to encourage children to investigate:
- Through quizzes and games.
- Through questions and instructions.
- Through research, enquiry and contributions to displays.
- Through the senses e.g. feeling, touching etc.
- Through manipulation; How was it made? How does it work? How is it used? etc.
- Through social interaction e.g. in role play areas and when collaborating in the production of images and models for display, etc.
- Through exploring the tools and materials that have been used by others to produce the work on display.

# Different Types of Display

If the following different categories are considered it will ensure that there is variety in the type of displays the children see, use and contribute to throughout the school year. The emphasis will however vary at times more towards one category than to others, e.g. at the start of a new project or topic.

- **Stimulus Displays** This type of display is designed to arouse interest in a particular concept or theme. It is usually created at the beginning of a new term or topic and is initially set up by the teacher with subsequent additions contributed by the children once the topic is underway.

- **Informative Displays** This type of display is designed to introduce knowledge, provide summaries of work or to reinforce learning. This category will also include notice boards for parents and visitors to inform them about 'out of school' activities, forthcoming events, details of the uniform etc.

- **Celebratory Displays** This type of display is designed to celebrate, and share children's work with a wider audience and to encourage further achievements.

- **Role Play Areas** These are display areas in themselves often created by the children whilst they play and in which the teacher can later intervene to extend learning in different areas of the curriculum.

- **Children's Display Areas** These are areas where the work on display has been trimmed, mounted, put up and labelled by the children. It takes courage to allow this type of display as initially it will be very different from other displays in school and may need a lot of support and guidance from the teacher!

These categories should not be seen or focused on in isolation. The most successful displays often contain elements of them all.

*Work on 'Tree Bark' celebrated with a wider audience.*

*A 'Stimulus Display' to arouse interest in letter sounds.*

## Tools

- **Rotary Trimmers** (often referred to as guillotines) These are safe and ideal for making straight cuts. Always push the paper to the top of the

*Using the guillotine to cut a straight edge.*

trimmer and against the raised ruled edge to keep it square. Push the outer edge under the plastic strip next to the blade and arrange the inner edge along one of the lines marked on the base of the trimmer. Hold the paper down firmly before sliding the blade along the plastic strip to ensure an accurate and straight cut. A large trimmer will be needed to cut big sheets of paper. If funds allow a small version is useful and more manageable when the paper to be cut is small.

- **Scissors** These are fine for most 'cut and stick' jobs provided they are of good quality and are in a good state of repair i.e. not blunt or with glue attached!

- **Safety Snips** These are ideal for cutting thick materials such as card, safely, where scissors might not suffice.

- **Stanley Knives and Cutting Mats** These knives are useful when used in conjunction with a safety ruler for cutting window mounts. Cutting should always be done on a cutting mat to avoid damaging the surface on which the card or paper is resting. They need to be carried and stored safely as they can be regarded as an offensive weapon!

- **Drawing Pins** These come in a variety of sizes and colours. Brass headed ones are better kept for notice board displays only as they can be a distraction when they shine amongst the work. Coloured versions are more successful especially if they are chosen to match the

mounts or the background on which the work is arranged.

- **Mapping Pins** These will fulfil the same purpose as drawing pins and likewise their coloured heads can be chosen to blend in with the work on display.

- **Dress Maker Pins** These are straight metal pins that can be used in conjunction with a pin push. Pushing them in individually by hand can result in very sore fingers!

- **Pin Push** This tool consists of a thin metal tube with a magnet inside it, attached to a plastic handle. A dress pin is inserted into the tube with the point facing outwards. The pin push is then placed in position on the work, and the handle pressed down firmly. The tube retracts slightly as the pin is pushed through the work into the display board to hold it in place. A second pin is then inserted and the pin push can be used again in the same way. It is an ideal tool for reaching and attaching things in awkward corners and for getting a firm attachment inside or behind a piece of 3D work.

- **Staple Guns** These are useful display tools but can be very temperamental! A metal gun tends to have more stamina than one that is a combination of metal and plastic. A heavy duty gun is VERY heavy and not an easy tool to use above shoulder height!

- **Staplers** A conventional stapler when opened up works quite well as an alternative to a staple gun.

- **Bambi Staplers** These work well as an alternative to adhesive when attaching work to a background mount.

- **Staple Extractors** Various types are available. They are useful for removing staples provided these are not too firmly embedded in the display board. This tends to happen if display boards are very soft.

- **A Steel Measuring Tape** Useful when organising straight lines within a display. A length of cotton thread can be pinned and used in a similar way.

- **Card Strips** For spacing work evenly (this will be explained fully later in the book).

- **Pens** Needed to add lettering to a display if the computer is not being used. Both thick and thin black felt tip pens are useful as the lettering will need to vary in size depending where it is positioned on the display e.g. headings, labels, questions, information etc.

- **Metallic Pencils** These are useful for writing on dark colours e.g. if the work is mounted on a dark background and children are to add their names or titles to their work.

- **Copydex** An impact adhesive that is useful when mounting heavy pieces of work. It sometimes causes papers to wrinkle as it dries. PVA glues also tend to act in a similar way.

- **Glue Sticks** Ideal for mounting light pieces of work.

- **Blu-tak.** A plastic adhesive useful for positioning work before it is pinned or stapled. If used as a permanent fixative it can bleed into the paper leaving oily stains. It can only hold a limited load and it is advisable to use a number of small pieces rather than big chunks.

- **Spray on Adhesives** (not shown here) These are quick and easy to use but are costly and tend to weaken in a warm atmosphere, in which case the work will peel off the mounts.

- **Velcro Tabs** (not shown here) Small pieces of sticky backed velcro that are attached to the back of the mount to attach it to a display board that has a flocked fabric covering.

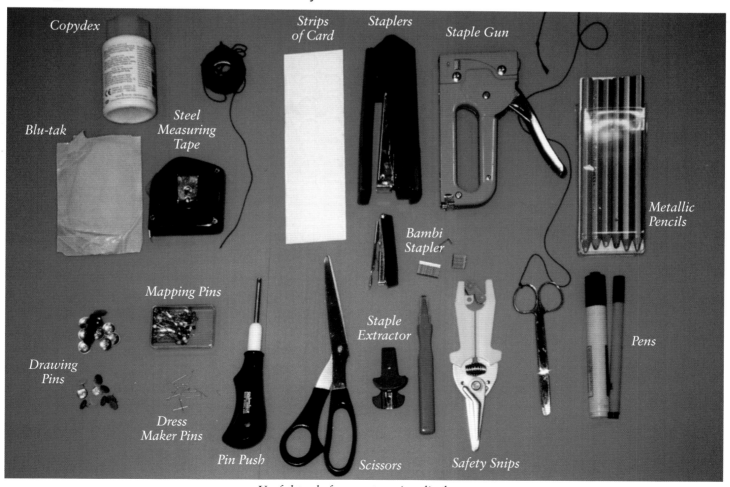

*Useful tools for constructing displays.*

# Papers

There is a wide range of different sorts of paper available on the market. It is a good idea to contact educational suppliers for swatches or samples of the different types of display papers available in their catalogues before purchasing. This will give you a better idea of the actual colours and the quality of the different papers.

- **Poster Paper** This is a popular paper for display as it comes in a range of bright colours either as sheets or on a roll and usually has a matt finish. It is available in single colour reams as well as assorted colours - particularly useful if there is to be a colour theme at Christmas. It does not fade easily and can therefore be used for several consecutive displays.
- **Sugar Paper** A rough textured paper that comes in a range of muted colours. It is available as sheets or on a roll. It tends to fade quickly and is therefore not easily re-usable.
- **Activity Paper** A paper with the qualities of sugar paper but in brighter and more vivid colours.
- **Pastel Paper** A double -sided paper that has a dark shade of a colour on one side and a lighter version of it on the reverse. It comes in a limited range of subtle colours.
- **Milskin** Tough embossed paper with a slightly shiny finish. Only available in rolls.
- **Corrugated Paper** Available in rolls and sheets. Useful for creating free standing bays for displays of work, zig -zag books or small table top screens.
- **Cardboard** Comes in a range of colours and thicknesses. 3-4 sheet thickness is ideal as a mounting card or for creating zig-zag books.

- **Border Rolls** Useful for dividing large boards into sections or to add an extra colour and impact around the edge of a display board. They come in a range of colours and finishes. e.g.
  a) Crepe paper border roll stretches, has a straight edge, is fairly tough and does not fade quickly.

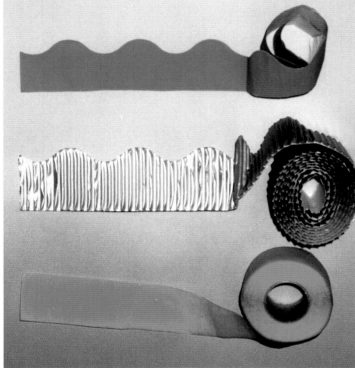

*Border Rolls - Crepe, corrugated and poster paper.*

  b) Poster paper border roll comes in a range of bright colours, has a wavy or straight edge which tends to curl up easily if leant against!
  c) Corrugated border roll comes either patterned or plain in a range of colours and styles, e.g. wavy edged, spiked, with a picket fence look etc. Patterned borders tend to be more limiting in their use if they are not going to detract from the subject of the display. They are strong, do not fade and are readily re-usable

## Paper Weights

The weight of papers and boards is determined by either grams per square metre (GSM) or in pounds per ream of 500 sheets - the heavier the weight the thicker the paper. Some boards have their thickness identified by a sheet thickness e.g. 4 sheet, 6 sheet etc. - the higher the number the heavier the weight.

## Paper Amounts

Paper / board may be bought by the
a)  Ream (480 sheets)
b)  Quire (24 sheets)
c)  Single sheets.
d)  Or by the roll.

## Paper Sizes

Papers are usually available in standard sizes determined by the International Standards Organisation (ISO).

The largest    **A0: 841 x 1189 mm**
                      **A1: 594 x 841 mm**
                      **A2: 420 x 594 mm**
                      **A3: 297 x 420 mm**
                      **A4: 210 x 297 mm**
The smallest   **A5: 148 x 210 mm**

A5 is usually the smallest size available. Many paper suppliers offer a free cutting service when paper is ordered. This can assist in having paper ready cut to size for mounting work and make the storing of paper in the stock cupboard more manageable.

# Drapes

Fabrics are undoubtedly valuable and versatile display materials however it is necessary to be discerning in the choice of colours and patterns to use in order to keep the focus on the display and not to distract from it. Polka dots and peacock feathers don't necessarily go well together! Too many 'draped' displays can create a fussy, complicated and cluttered effect rather than impact. It is unwise to trail lengths of old curtains around children's work hoping that this will make the display more effective!

*Drapes used to disguise boxes creating different levels.*

Plain fabrics are usually more versatile than patterned ones as they tend to enhance the subject matter better by not distracting the eye. Fabric samples, off-cuts and end of rolls can often be picked up at a reasonable price from dress and furnishing departments. Jumble sales likewise are a good source of supply.

Points in the favour of fabrics are:
- They can be effective in hiding pipes, switches and other eyesores that are all too often adjacent to or even run across a display board.
- They can cover and disguise boxes used to create different levels within a display of objects to be handled, books or 3D work.
- They are durable and re-usable and are easily added to a display.

Remember though that not every display needs a drape - less is best!

Fabrics can also be displayed for their own qualities rather than as backdrops for other items.
- They can be used to show examples of different techniques e.g. batik, patchwork, weaving, felting and tie-dying etc.
- They can be used to make cross cultural links with traditions from other parts of the world e.g. bold prints from Africa, richly embroidered Sari fabrics, Shisha mirror work, Indian block prints, Scottish tartan etc.
- They can be used as a stimulus to show different ways of producing pattern using the same starting point e.g. patterns made up of stripes that use different widths and colours in a variety of ways.
- If several versions of the same fabric design are displayed they can show how a design can seem to alter in appearance when different colours are used.
- Fabrics can also be displayed for their scientific interest e.g. natural fabrics and their sources, man-made fabrics and the process of their manufacture.

Fabrics when displayed in their own right offer a good basis for cross-curricular work involving a wide range of skills including maths, language and the humanities etc. They can become a display in their own right and not just an addition to a display.

*A drape linked to the content of the display.*

# Colour Schemes

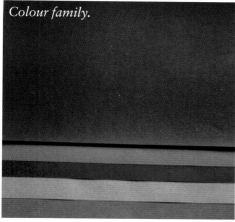

*Colour family.*

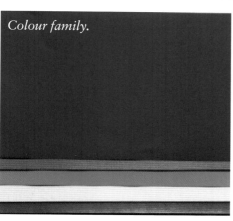

*Colour family.*

Colour plays an important part in the general impression and feel of a building and the choice of colours used in display can greatly enhance or detract from how we feel about, react to, enjoy and appreciate the learning environment that we are in. Dark areas need light colours. Cold areas need warm colours and consideration should be given to the linking of separate areas using colour e.g. adjacent boards, boards down the length of a corridor, around a resource area or around the hall.

Colour can unite a group of displays that have a similar theme or even a variety of themes. Too many variations of colour in a small area can detract from rather than enhance the work on show. The aim should be for a bright, cheerful, interesting and uncluttered area where it is enjoyable to work.

When choosing colour for backing a board or for mounting work many factors come into play and need to be considered. Not least of these is 'what is available in the stock cupboard'! Towards the end of the financial year and before the new stock is ordered the choice may be limited and

*Colour family.*

much ingenuity needed. This is a time when the pile of dull looking sugar paper that has been stockpiling for years can be useful!

Muted shades work well when used as a background for work mounted on bright colours or vice- versa. Two strong colours together in a display can

*Colour family.*

result in an excess of colour at the expense of the work on show e.g. consider bright purple and orange together! Fluorescent papers are best used sparingly - if at all! They tend to dominate a display and are hard on the eye. They work well on notice boards as they draw the eye to the information to be read.

If the paper for display purposes is kept in a stock cupboard at a distance from the classroom it is often difficult to remember what papers are available and which colours work well together. There might be the ideal choice for the display in progress - if only you knew they were there! To help decision making and to save time i.e. making the wrong choice of colours which then need to be returned to the stock cupboard, keep a small swatch of all the display papers available to you in the classroom area. This will give you the opportunity to try different colours together next to the work before it is mounted and displayed and will save time and effort when visiting the stock cupboard itself.

We learn a lot from how other people combine and use colour. To collect and save ideas it is a good idea to photograph completed displays both within your own school and in other schools when you visit - after asking permission of course! This collection of visual images will be a useful source of ideas for future displays as well as showing possible ways of utilizing space - and may offer solutions for utilizing more effectively those awkward areas within the school environment.

When choosing colours on which to mount and display work the content or theme of the display will often provide prompts, particularly if the topic is seasonal. A winter topic will look better on blue, grey and white rather than red, green and yellow!

Try not to combine too many colours on a board - one for the background one for the mounts and a possible third as a border. If the work is to be double mounted a neutral colour such as black or grey works well as the first mount with colour for the second one. Make sure the colour you have chosen for the mounts looks good with the background. Too much colour and it will overpower the work. Too little or too similar colours and it will be unexciting and uninteresting. Two colours from the same colour family can work well together provided one is stronger and bolder than the other.

*Examples of colours that work together.*

Some suggestions for colour schemes:
- **Black and white** always looks effective and are usually available.
- Add **red** as a background colour and grey as a second mount to extend this colour scheme.
- **Grey** is subtle and works well for historical projects.
- **Earth colours / Natural colours** e.g. brown, green, grey and cream fade very little and are sympathetic with natural / observational work.
- Bright **red/ yellow and black** glow and will create an exciting display area.
- **Brown, yellow and gold** provide a mellow warm colour scheme.
- **Green and blue** are crisp and fresh - try yellow instead of green with blue for a similar effect.

- **Purple and pink** provide a rich background and may need grey or black as a second mount for interest.
- **Orange and brown** work well together as do grey and blue.

If art work is to be displayed, ideas for the colour scheme could be linked to and taken from the work itself. If decisions are to be made unrelated to a specific topic or theme try working around and with the existing room colours e.g. chairs, walls, doors, curtains, storage units etc.

Further examples of colour schemes are included in the illustrations - they are by no means all the possibilities and are only suggestions.

Examples of coloured backgrounds with single and double mounts.
(Children's work is represented by white squares.)

*Double mount on a purple background.*

*Double mount on a pale blue background.*

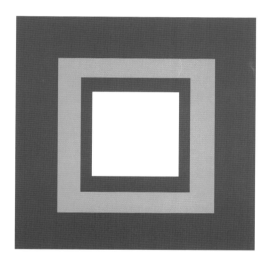

*Double mount on a blue background.*

*Single yellow mount on a blue background.*

*Single mount on a brown background.*

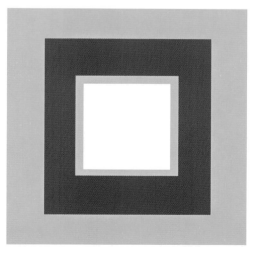

*Double mount on an orange background.*

## Getting Started

Once the colour scheme has been decided on, the board can be backed in the chosen colour. Before doing this it is a good idea to check:

- That you have selected sufficient backing paper from the stock cupboard to cover the whole of the display board. It is easy to make a mistake and to find that you are a few sheets short of the number actually needed. It is also most frustrating to find that, on returning to the stock cupboard, there is none of the original colour left on the shelf. Decision making in this case now has to start all over again!

- That you have a staple gun that works and that it is full of staples! It is very annoying to run out, particularly when you are standing on steps and are just about to fasten the final piece of backing paper to the board. There never seems to be any one around when this happens and as you climb down from your perch in search of more staples that last piece of paper seems to have a mind of its own and decides to descend to the floor as well!

- That the staple gun has a piece of cardboard attached to its under surface - but not covering the hole where the staples come out. This is to push the staple gun slightly away from the board and leave each staple, when fired, with a slight lip sticking out. This will make staple extraction very easy and safe, particularly if the display boards are soft and the staple gun fires them deeply into the board. This slight lip doesn't detract at all from the appearance of the display,

- That as you pick up the paper to use for backing (if it is in sheet form) you always keep the same side of each sheet facing the front. This aims to prevent a chequer board effect occurring that possibly isn't

intended or wanted and will in fact detract from the final display. Even following this sequence doesn't guarantee that sometimes the sheets of paper don't exactly match which is most annoying!

- That the backing paper lies flat and level on the board - if it looks messy and creased before the mounted work is added it won't be improved by the pieces of work themselves and the whole display will suffer as a consequence. Try to position the staples you use, to run, as far as possible, in the same direction. This will be less distracting from the overall appearance of the display.

- Attach the border - if you are going to use one - at this stage as it will give an indication of the space now available on the board for the pieces of work and how they can be arranged, and not crammed, into this space.

- If the display board is small it can be extended by attaching more of the same backing paper to the wall on either side of the board. Small pieces of Blu - tak will be needed to attach the paper and the mounted work added will need to be small and light so that it doesn't pull the backing paper away from the wall.

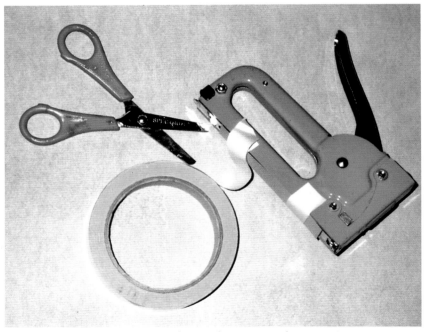

*Preparing your staple gun for easy staple extraction.*

# Mounting

Any work on display should be shown off clearly and simply. One of the most important ways of doing this is through the sensitive use of colour and tone as discussed previously. Another is by the way the work is mounted. Careful attention when mounting work can raise its profile, similarly lack of care can detract from the work and make it appear inferior.

There are several different ways of mounting work:

## Single Mounting

This can be quick and effective and proportion is the key to its success. Small pieces of work need a reasonably wide mount to give them status and focus, large pieces of work speak for themselves and a narrow mount will suffice. A single mount can look attractive and more effective with a fine black line drawn around the picture a little way from the edge.

*Small piece of work on a single wide mount.*

*Large piece of work on a narrow single mount.*

It is often suggested in books and guidance on display that the margin at the bottom of a mount should be greater in proportion. Work mounted square i.e. where all the margins are equal can look, in my opinion, equally effective. This rule applies to both displays of written and illustrative work and to displays that are a mixture of both.

*Small piece of work on a double mount. Note the different widths used.*

## Double Mounting

Double mounting is when two mounts, an inner and an outer one, are used one on top of the other. The inner and the outer mount can be of contrasting colours, two tones of the same colour or a neutral (black or grey) with a colour.

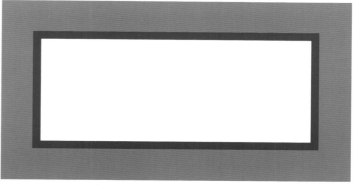

*Large piece of work on a double mount. Again, note the different widths used.*

Considering the proportion of the mounts is again important. If the first mount is fairly wide then the second one will be more effective if it is not identical i.e. it needs to be narrow. If the first mount is narrow the opposite will apply.

## Triple Mounting

A triple mount is when three mounts of varying widths are used - it is effective but if this method is used it will takes considerable time to do and uses a lot of paper in the process.

If you intend gluing work to a mount remember some adhesives can cause paper to crinkle and ruin the effect. Stapling mounts and work together is an alternative, quick and professional approach. If the staples used are small and positioned discreetly to run in the same direction and in line with the work itself they will be unobtrusive. This is also more economical than gluing as the mounts can be used again.

*Work with a triple mount.*

## Unmounted Work

Unmounted work can look good if there is a strong contrast between the work itself and the background e.g. black on yellow. The pieces of work need to be carefully and closely trimmed and arranged as a cluster on the board to unify them as a group. Ensure that the spacing between the work is even and that the title is strong and bold.

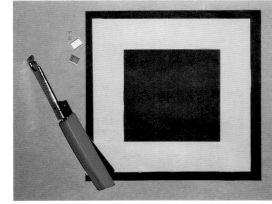

*Mount stapled instead of glued.*

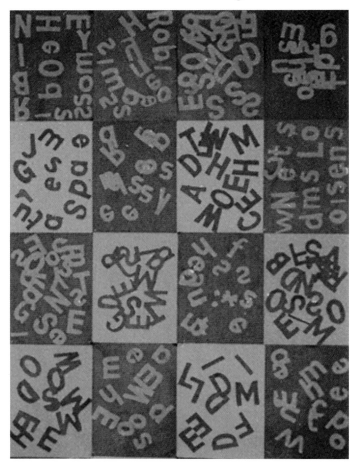

*Unmounted work.*

## Window Mounts

This consists of placing windows or frames cut from card or strong paper over the work. The advantage is that the frames can be used several times. However, such frames take time to produce and need to be measured and cut accurately.

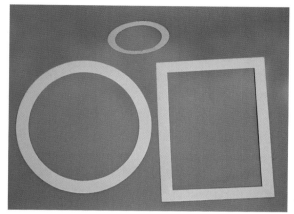

They work well in focusing the attention on the achievement in a piece of work whilst disguising the mechanics e.g. untidy edges in a piece of textile work. Samples of ready cut window mounts can be purchased from various educational catalogues and are useful to keep as templates for when such mounts need to be drawn and cut for display.

They are also sometimes available from local photographers and picture framers free of charge, particularly if they are soiled or marked in some way and therefore unsaleable - it is worth enquiring. These too would be useful to be kept as templates for future use.

*Window mounts.*

## Picture Frames

Purchased frames e.g. of the clip frame variety, are useful for displaying work in traffic areas e.g. corridors or stairways. They are ideal for creating a school gallery particularly if photos of the artists/ authors are displayed next to the work with information about them. You will need to make sure the frames are hung securely and that perspex is used rather than glass.

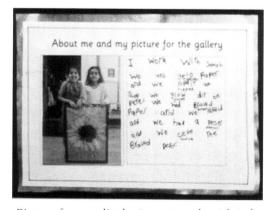

*Picture frames displaying artwork with information about the artists.*

# Planning and Arranging the Layout

The essence of good display is the control and effective use of space. The aim is to catch the eye and invite it to investigate further and absorb and appreciate the information presented. This works well if we create a sense of direction and balance within a display.

Keep things simple! The more fussy a display becomes the more it loses its message. If work is on a rectangular / square piece of paper then it needs to be presented horizontally. Try laying the work on the floor beneath the board 'brick style' with verticals, horizontals and parallels fitting simply together.

Work with the shape of the board - most display boards are rectangular or square in shape (even if they are hung in awkward spots and at undesirable heights) Key Stage Two may get large boards down to floor level and end up putting pieces of furniture in front of them whereas Key Stage One may get boards that are small and way above the children's heads!

When arranging the work run it parallel with the edges of the board and leave a border around the work as a breathing space. Work will look better and create more of a focus if it is in a tight block with limited space between each piece, rather than filling the board and leaving large gaps between each one.

# Spacing

To help make decisions about the amount of space to allow between the pieces of work it is a good idea to have a box full of strips of card of varying widths. Try these different widths of card between the pieces of work whilst it is lying on the floor in order to choose spacing that will allow the maximum amount of work to fit evenly and effectively on the board. Hold the card 'spacer' between the pieces of work as you attach them to the board and the spacing will be even and regular.

If you try arranging work by attaching it temporarily with Blu-tak it may well come adrift before you have time to fasten it down. Mapping pins are more effective in this situation.

*Strips of card used to create equal spaces between pieces of work.*

## Straight Lines

If work is following the shape of the board it will need to run in straight lines. Almost straight and travelling up the board should be avoided at all costs. Never ask a friend 'Is it straight?' whilst you are standing close to the work as they will say 'yes' possibly without looking! They are busy people too, and once you are able to view the work at a distance you may realise it is not as straight as you intended.

If you are unsure about creating straight lines at the top, along the middle or at the side of a group of work, pin a piece of cotton across or down the board where you want the straight line to be, as a guide. Make sure this is pinned up straight before you begin fastening the work parallel to it!

*Using straight lines to follow the shape of a board.*

Using the cotton and the card spacers should aid greater accuracy when arranging work on a board. You may not need this support if you have a good eye for straight lines. Providing the first piece of work is straight the others can be lined up, by eye, to follow on. If the first one is slightly crooked and the next one is is lined up to match it, the display may well end up meandering up the board and be far from straight! If there is a sloping ceiling next to the board you may need to arrange the work at a slight angle to fool the eye and make it appear that it is straight!

Teachers are often tempted to arrange work at different angles or to dot it around on a board - this can distract from the display and confuse the viewer. If you wish to do something different or unusual have fun with the title of the display, not with the work itself. Art work is never hung at angles in galleries to create interest!

There are occasions when, however, it is appropriate to put work up at different angles but not when the child has selected a rectangular piece of paper which has become the whole painting all of which is seen by them as important and necessary.

## Trimming

Work needs to be carefully cut to have straight edges using a trimmer before it is mounted. Some teachers have a tendency to 'cut round' the child's work, keeping the 'best bits' and discarding the rest before adding it unmounted to a display. Once part of a painting has been removed the quality is in danger of being destroyed and it becomes something different. Any picture 'cut out' has a curious cloudlike quality to its shape. In any picture the background is as important as the foreground or central figure. Children need to be encouraged to see the 'composition' of a picture as being important. If part of the picture is removed it suggests that it does not matter.

There are times when it is appropriate to cut round children's work e.g. when we are combining lots of individual and independent units for a class frieze. Similarly if the child isn't considering the whole piece of paper but merely painting a single item on it e.g. a face or a flower head - then it might be a good idea to cut the single objects out and even arrange them at irregular angles.

## Arranging

Many teachers burn the 'midnight oil' when putting a display together. Any display takes considerable time and effort to assemble successfully and is often done at the end of a long and busy working day. Time spent in this way is not wasted. However, the children won't necessarily spend much time looking at such a complete display the next day and may even need encouragement to notice it and observe it fully. An incomplete display although not to everyone's liking will have a more positive response e.g. What's going there? Where is my piece of work? Sheer nosiness, enquiry and involvement in their environment has been aroused. They want to know just what is going on and what is going to happen next! Try adding a little more to the display each day and the curiosity should continue and the display itself assume considerable importance.

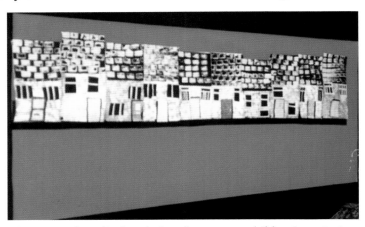

*An incomplete display designed to arouse children's curiosity.*

## The Children's Own Display Board

In some schools, where there is space, children have been given a display board on which they can arrange work that they have mounted. It takes courage to do this as the initial results may be a bit bizarre. However it is a way of appreciating and sharing the children's interests and ideas for their learning environment. Help, tact and suggestions will need to be available.

## Showing the Sequence

Work which displays topics or themes in sequence may need to include arrows, coloured tape or string to invite the participation of the onlooker and lead them through the display.

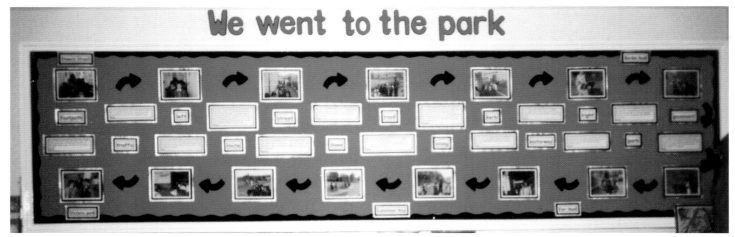

*Arrows used to show the sequence of a display.*

# Displaying the Process and the Product

Where possible and appropriate, displays should ideally show the process followed, as well as celebrating the children's achievements.

*Comments by the children about what they have achieved.*

I like the beard because it looks real. I got some wool and cut them the same size, I got some 3D paint underneath then glued the wool on.

*Comments by the children about what they have achieved.*

To do this a display of children's work may need to show the following:

- The source material used to generate the work e.g. photographs, objects, web site addresses, books etc.
- Preliminary drawings and notes made by the children to investigate ideas about starting points and resources.
- Finished work by a number of children to illustrate the range of achievement.
- Explanatory notes might be needed to engage the onlooker and add further information.
- Comments by the children about what they have achieved.

Where such displays are on view either in public areas or classrooms within the school, they should generate discussion about the work both by children and colleagues. They can also inform parents, visitors, and governors about the nature and purpose of the work that is being undertaken in school.

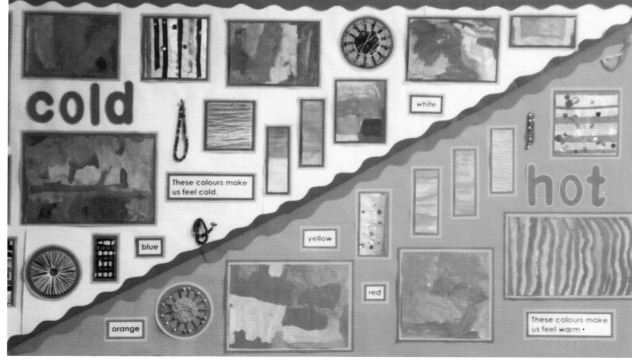

*Display which includes both process and end product.*

## Selecting work for Display

It is important that every child in the class should have some of his/her work on show during the school term. However it is appreciated that the amount of display space available is quite likely to provide constraints and limitations to this.

The problem of the talented child's / children's work constantly being on show to the exclusion of others is that although the displays will look stunning, other children in the group may feel discouraged and undervalued and that their efforts are in fact inadequate.

The selection of work should therefore be based not only on the outward appearance of each piece of work but on the teacher's knowledge of the individual child and his/ her progress and effort. On occasions the teacher may display the entire work of the class whilst at other times the children could be encouraged to select their own pieces of work. If this is the case and display space is at a premium try mounting and arranging some of the work on the display board and mount the rest of it in a flip chart style book. Hang this book in the middle of the display board and every day turn a page and discuss the new work on show. This will allow the work of each child to be seen at some time whilst the display is on the board.

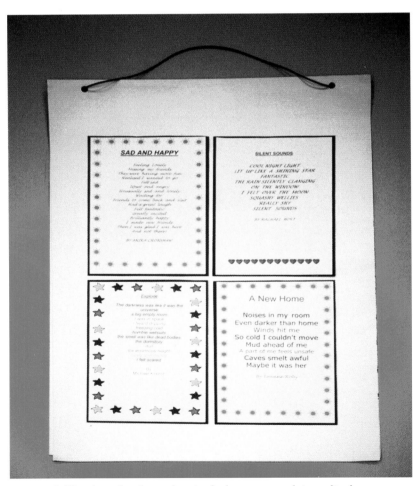

*A flip chart book used to include more work in a display.*

The building and organisation of displays needs to be seen as part of the children's learning experience and they should be given plenty of opportunity to become involved in and to discuss what goes on show and how it is displayed.

## The Layout

Several examples of different ways of arranging work follow, plus points to consider in each case. These are by no means the only arrangements that can and should be used. Much will depend on the shape of the boards to be used and the size, shape and quantity of work to be displayed. They should be seen only as ideas and suggestions for a variety of arrangements, some of which may be new or may stimulate ways of displaying work that have not been used or considered in the past.

In the arrangements the white shapes represent the children's work and the grey areas represent the display boards. Lettering and labels have been omitted but space has been left for these to be incorporated.

# Regular Arrangements

In regular arrangements the work must be on pieces of paper of the same size and care must be taken to cut all the mounts either square or rectangular.

Aim for a nicely balanced arrangement with the work evenly spaced in straight lines - avoid dotting the work about randomly.

Spacing is crucial. It must be even and fairly close. Arrange the work in a tight group in the middle of the board with a small space of equal size between each individual piece - use a strip of card as a spacer. Too much space and the work will look as if it is floating

*A regular arrangement.*

and trying desperately to fill the board rather than having impact. Leave a much wider border around the work, between the group and the edge of the display board. This will invite the viewer to focus first on the whole group before investigating the individual pieces.

# Hanging on a Line

In this arrangement the work displayed varies in size. When positioning the work on the board keep the tops of the pieces of work level and in a straight line using a piece of cotton as a guide. The bottoms of the work can be of any height as long as a breathing space remains below them. If the

larger pieces of the work are in the centre of the group they will provide a focus whilst the smaller pieces will balance the arrangement and lead the eye to the outer edges.

The title of such a display could be placed above the group using the row of work to underline it.

## A Reflective Arrangement

In this arrangement the work varies in size and is arranged above and below a central space that creates a straight line along which the eye will travel. Balance the work so that pieces of similar size match and reflect each other.

As in the previous arrangement place the larger pieces in the centre of the display with the smaller pieces at the outer edges. Leave a small breathing space around the work. Keep the spacing between the work even and tight.

*A reflective arrangement.*

## Work Arranged Around a Title

In this arrangement the pieces of work which vary in size are grouped around the title of the display. The outer edges of the work need to be kept in line to create an even rectangle all the way round. An irregular breathing space forms the centre of the display around the title whilst an even space surrounds the outside of the group to create a focus.

*Work arranged around a title.*

## Scale and Balance within an Arrangement

Scale is important. Here the larger, main pieces of work are supported by smaller ones. The aim is to achieve a balance of large and small within the arrangement. Position any written or detailed pieces of work at eye level or towards the bottom of the display so that they can easily be read.

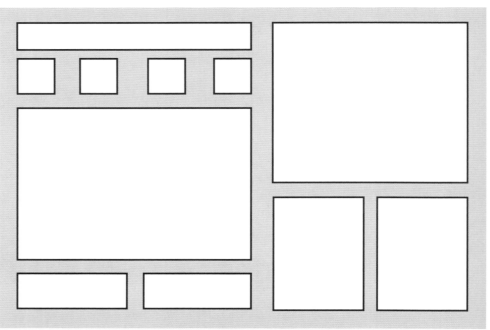

*Balance and scale used in an arrangement.*

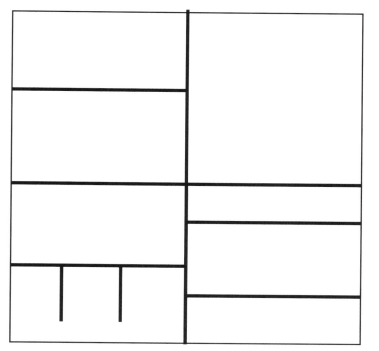

## Irregular Arrangements

Arrangements of pieces of work which are different shapes and sizes always present a challenge. In order to produce a unified arrangement the pieces of work must be fitted closely together in a cluster - remembering to keep spacing even. To prevent the cluster of work from looking haphazard, strong vertical and horizontal 'lines of balance' need to be established. Lines of balance provide a framework on which the work can hang. They give the display order and stability. Imagine them as a strong vertical tree with several horizontal offshoots e.g.

Select one piece of work. Put this up first and relate the others to it giving the arrangement a focal point. Place the strongest shapes to the centre and the smaller pieces further out. Try not to overcrowd the board. Leave a good breathing space all around the edges and keep spaces between the work even. Each time this type of arrangement is undertaken it will be different

*Irregular arrangement based on 'Patterns From Fruit'.*

# Displaying 3D work

The display of 3D work presents its own problems - mainly because it is often of a fragile nature and there is limited space in which to display it. Many classrooms have hardly enough room for the children, never mind a splendid display! Improvisation is usually necessary to create a 3D display in the classroom. Such displays are often done on a surface in front of a display board if space is available. Three dimensional and two dimensional work can then be related and links made between the two if required. A zig-zag book/ screen made from folded card placed behind the display is another way of linking the two and providing information about the work.

As with two dimensional displays there are approaches for displaying three dimensional objects that will enhance an arrangement and ensure a more coherent display. A collection of items placed on a continuous flat surface can on occasions resemble a jumble sale rather than a display and as a result become a dumping ground for lunch boxes, books etc. If a continuous flat surface is to be used the objects on display will have more impact if they are each placed on an individual paper plate covered, if required, with pieces of paper that match the backing paper on the wall behind the display. Ideally 3D objects need to be displayed on

different levels. These can be created in a variety of ways, all of which are quick and easy to assemble.

## Boxes and Stands

*A group of different shaped boxes unified by colour.*

A set of boxes in various sizes covered in either black or white paper or sticky backed plastic will be an asset for any display area. The group of boxes will look better if unified by one colour. If necessary cover the combined group with a cloth to create a continuous run of the same colour. It will help simplify the storage of such boxes if they are of sizes that will fit inside one another.

There are also many clean shaped boxes in polystyrene that come as packaging around electrical goods and may be neutral in colour and not need covering. Stage blocks are another alternative. However, these are only a temporary and short term solution as they may be needed for class assemblies etc. which means hurriedly dismantling a display.

*3D figures displayed on paper plates.*

The tops of such a group of boxes can look effective if covered with cork tiles or squares of hessian.

## Tubes or Tins

When covered with paper or sticky backed plastic, coffee tins or cardboard tubes can be made into really professional looking resources and cost little or nothing to make. It is however important to cover them carefully and as before unite the group by colour. Circles of card on the top of each tube or tin will add to the appearance of the display and give a broader surface on which to place the objects.

Broad strips of corrugated card rolled into tubes make a base for lightweight displays. These too

need a circle of card on top of them to become more substantial display areas. Such tubes and circles can also be arranged in tiers if different heights are required.

When arranging a display on a group of boxes or tubes, objects should be grouped according to bulk and height. Obviously the longest and the tallest will be placed at the back or bottom of the display enabling

smaller items to be seen. Avoid arranging boxes or objects in straight rows. Place them instead at different heights and distances from the observer.

*Attaching tiles to a display using copydex.*

## Stands

The free standing wire display stands such as those used for displaying books are useful when displaying flat clay tiles which are fragile and easily broken. Such tiles can also be displayed by first attaching them with Copydex to a piece

*Covered tins or tubes.*

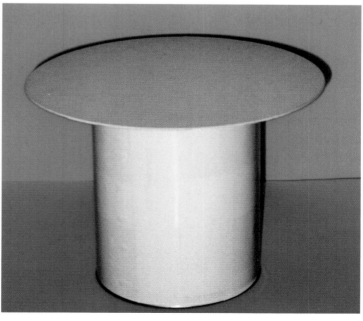

27

of card and then fastening the card to the display board. If tiles have a hole made at the top before they are allowed to dry, they can be hung on the display board using a pin push and straight dressmaker pins.

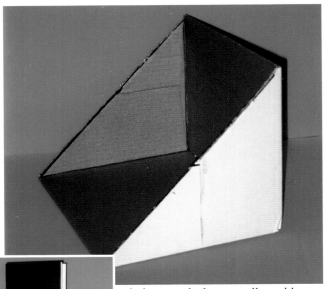

*Shelves made from cardboard boxes.*

## Shelves

All schools need shelving for a wide variety of storage and display. Often these are not adjacent to a display board or in an area appropriate for display. Simple, temporary shelves can be made using house bricks and pieces of wood or discarded shelves.

Simple shelves to include books, models and stimulus material can easily be made by cutting diagonally down the sides of a box that held A4 photocopying paper and removing the front of it. Such shelves can be attached to the wall either upright or in reverse depending on what is going on them and enable a combination of 2D and 3D material to be combined in the same display. To unify the display cover the shelves with paper that matches the board itself.

Shelves across window recesses can also be successful. Not only are the objects protected by the recess but they are set off by the advantage of the daylight behind them.

## Lighting

Wherever work or resources are displayed objects need to be seen clearly and the positioning of displays needs consideration. Special lighting is expensive but can make all the difference when long dark corridors are used for display. Spotlights and tracking systems once installed are easy to maintain. They can swivel into new positions to highlight work that might otherwise merge into the gloom, so making hitherto little used areas dynamic, vital and far more useful.

## Safety

When attaching 3D objects to the wall or placing them on shelves make sure that the shelves are secure and that any breakable objects can be viewed safely - this of course may mean placing them where they can not be handled. When dress maker pins are used make sure they don't protrude at the children's eye level.

When storing a box of such pins, pin the lid of the box to the base using a couple of pins - this will mean the top and the bottom of the box will not part company when you grab it off the shelf in a hurry and scatter pins all over the place!

Consider where displays are sighted particularly if they are in a traffic area. The lunch queue may not be sympathetic to a display that protrudes too far out from the wall. Similarly if a display is arranged at a low level or uses floor space, consider whether it may become an obstacle which is easily tripped over. If it is, it will not remain a pristine, intact display for long.

Once a display is complete whether it is 2D or 3D stand back from it and look at the surrounding area. If this is messy or untidy - and we are all busy people with good intentions who are often overtaken by time and the pressure of work, it will distract considerably from all the hard work and effort that has been put into the display. Tidy up and your efforts will be viewed as you want them to be and much more appreciated.

*Examples of 3D work on display.*

Lettering is often the problematic part of display and is something that needs to be carefully considered when planning any part of the learning environment. It needs to be clear and effective and enhance a display rather than detract from it. Attractive displays can easily be spoilt by poorly formed, inappropriately placed lettering of the wrong scale.

There are three fundamental uses of lettering:

- the teacher putting up labels and headings to arouse interest in a display.
- the teacher adding information about the stimulus, resources and content of the display
- the child's written response to questions within the display or comments about the display and the work undertaken.

There are many methods of lettering that are within the scope of most teachers.

- Hand written lettering using felt tip pens
- Stencils and letter templates usually made of plastic or wood
- Computer text
- Use of the overhead projector
- Use of the photocopier
- Commercial pre - printed letters

The aim should always be for:

- Readability
- Simple captions
- Even lettering
- Labels in proportion

*Examples of different types of display lettering.*

**Readability** – Consider the position of the lettering on the display in order that it can be read easily. Try standing back to judge this. If the writing is positioned high up use bold, cut out letters or letters written using a thick pen. Take care that the letters blend with the display but are not 'lost'.

**Simple Captions** – Link titles and captions closely to the subject matter and keep writing to a minimum for maximum impact.

**Labels in Proportion** – Ensure that labels on display are smaller in size than the title so that they do not vie with the eye for attention. Watch that the lettering is also correspondingly thinner. If objects are part of a display make sure their labels are firmly attached. They can easily get lost leaving the display with little or muddled information on it.

Lettering should be legible, clear and concise. Within a display the lettering may have several purposes e.g. to Instruct, Warn, Advise, Control, Direct, Identify, Persuade, Announce, Decorate, Remind, Advertise, Commemorate or Command. The form or style of lettering chosen will of course largely depend on the nature and content of the display itself.

## Hand Written Lettering

When hand lettering it is advisable to rule lines or work on graph paper to keep the letters even - five squares high and three wide for most letters achieves good results.

If larger lettering is required use the photocopier

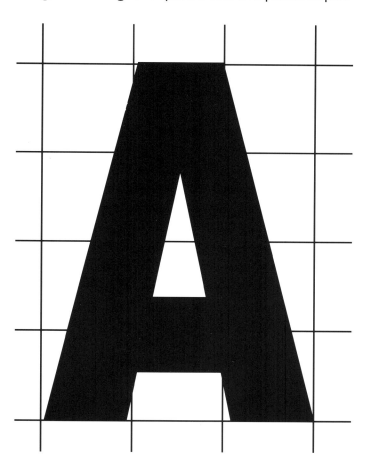

to enlarge them.

Felt pens with chisel tips offer the greatest possibilities as they allow maximum flexibility of line width.

When using ruled guide lines draw them with a gap of 3/4/3 unit intervals.

The letter ' T ' may be smaller than the other large letters. Make guide lines very feint then rub them out. Letters need space. When letters have straight sides it is quite easy to space them evenly, but if a letter is not straight-sided and equal space is left between, then the letter seems to be isolated because there is too much space around it. To solve this, bring the two letters either side a little closer, so that the letters now appear more equally spaced.

The simple rule for spacing words is to leave enough space for the letter 'o' between them e.g.

## TheОSunОisОShining

## Stencils and Letter Templates

The use of commercially produced wooden or plastic letter templates helps to raise the standard of lettering in displays. They give a degree of uniformity to headings and captions. The use of these throughout a school establishes a 'house style' with which the children become familiar and, which encourages them to recognise and read the words that are part of the displays. Stencils or templates need to be in several sizes as boards and display spaces vary in size and height. A large board in a large area e.g. the hall needs large lettering to grab the eye, whereas a small

*Stencils and letter templates.*

board within a classroom needs lettering that is smaller in size and less dominant. Some displays will require lettering in a variety of sizes e.g. a main heading in large letters, sub-headings in slightly smaller letters and finally captions and information in letters that are smaller again.

Letters should be clear and simple. One colour lettering which stands out against the backing paper is best. Black or white lettering is 'safe' but any colour that co-ordinates with the backing will be fine. Cut out letters can help carry colour through a display especially if the letters are matched to the mounting paper used round the pieces of work.  Letter templates can also be drawn round and cut from colour pictures or wrapping paper related to the subject or from fabric or painted or printed paper-careful cutting skills are required!

If two identical letters are cut from contrasting colours and one is slightly off-set, shadow lettering is created that gives depth and a three dimensional effect.
Edging letters are another way of using templates. Letters are drawn round and cut out of one paper then stuck down on to a contrasting paper. An even edge is then drawn round each letter before they are cut out a second time.

## Freely Cut Letter Shapes

On occasion letter shapes of your own design may be required e.g. when template  or stencil letter shapes would not match a theme e.g. spiky letters for a winter display. These letters will need to be of a similar height and this is often difficult to achieve when randomly cutting with no outline to follow. To overcome this problem, decide  how tall you want the letters to be and cut a long strip of paper to match this chosen height. Now as you cut your letters from this strip make sure each letter touches the top and bottom of the strip and they should end up similar in height and match one another as they form words on the display.

*Freely cut letter shapes.*

*Display using computer generated lettering.*

## Computer Text

A wide variety of fonts is available. Some are more legible than others so you need to be selective. Fonts that look attractive can sometimes be difficult to read. e.g.

# Display Display Display Display Display

There is no limit to the variety of styles and designs which can be adopted, however a suitable style is important for the message or information you wish to convey e.g. a display on space travel would look strange accompanied by gothic lettering.

Children can be encouraged to develop and use their IT skills and contribute to displays by typing captions and question. The use of a designated font will ensure that these are easily read. This is an ideal means of adding the children's names neatly to the pieces of work on display without detracting from the overall effect. It is important that children have ownership of their work on display and it is equally important that work displayed in corridors and halls can be identified and matched either to the class or children that produced it and to enable the children involved to be congratulated. The size of the font needed will also need investigation as size and proportion matter. e.g.

**A a   Point size 12**

# A a   Point size 24
# A a   Point size 48

## Use of the Overhead Projector
Look out for interesting lettering or titles. Trace over their outline on a transparency and project the image onto card pinned on the wall where it can again be drawn round before being cut out. Different sizes of  lettering  can be achieved by moving the projector nearer to or further from the wall.

## Use of the Photocopier
This will likewise allow interesting lettering or titles to be copied, scaled up or scaled down according to need.

## Commercial Pre-Printed Letters
These are available in a variety of sizes and colours and are on the whole flimsy and intended for single use only. Some are self-adhesive, others come in perforated sheets from which they are easily punched out and attached to the display with Blu-tak or staples. They come as both upper and lower case letters and are standard in size.

Where the title is not centrally placed on the display it is often effective to mount the letters on a separate paper background first before fastening it in position on the display. When doing this attach the centre letter first and work left and right, spacing the letters evenly, but not too far apart. e.g.
By adding questions and labels to a display the aim is to arouse interest and stimulate enquiry. These

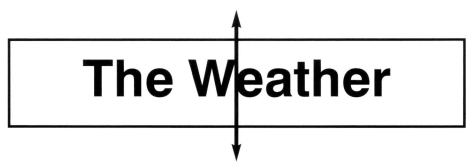

# Questions and Interaction

*Questions encourage children to interact with a display.*

need to use appropriate vocabulary and to be placed at a level so that they can be easily read by the target audience. This is not always an easy task as the amount of wall space at children's eye level in the classroom is limited. Children do not readily look up so it may be a wise ploy not to overload the display with too many captions or questions initially. Introduce a few at a time at eye level so that the children can touch them, read them and once they are familiar with these, move them further up or above the display and introduce more new captions and questions again at eye level. This will mean that although there is a lot of writing on different parts of the display and at different levels the children have viewed all of it and become familiar with it at eye level first.

Interaction with a display can be encouraged in a number of ways e.g. through questions, through quizzes, competitions and games, through the senses (how does it feel, taste, smell, sound) or through physical manipulation of objects (arranging or adding to collections, completing the other half of a picture, finding out how something works, investigating an object closely using a magnifying glass etc.)

All types of interaction demand a response or answer and there needs to be a means for the onlooker to do so. The response could be approached in a variety of ways e.g.

- A box for suggestions about the titles, or questions to be added to a display.
- Postcards or post-it notes on which the answers to questions together with the child's name could be written – these could then be collected and checked by the teacher and added to a book about the topic on display.
- A 'visitors book' in which the onlooker is invited to write comments about the display.
- A blank sheet of paper adjacent to the display on which the onlooker can record answers and comment (including their name).
- A tape recorder to record ideas.

Questions need to be carefully worded so that the intention is clear and phrased in such a way that the children have ownership of their answers e.g. what do you think…? Avoid those that can be answered with a simple yes or no.

**Examples of questions for stimulus displays might include:**

* What is the rest like? (a broken or incomplete object)
* What is it used for? (artefact)
* How does it work? (artefact)
* Do you like it? Why? (poem, music, painting, sound, something to smell or taste)
* What will happen next (picture, photograph, experiment).
* What is happening outside the picture frame?
* How does it make you feel? (poem, music, picture)
* What can we do about this? (emotive issues e.g.pollution)
* How likely? How many? (mathematics, problem solving)

* Which is your favourite and why?
* Which is your least favourite and why?
* Where does it come from? How do you know?
* Is it old or new? How do you know?
* What tools /technique has the artist used? etc.

Make sure the types of questions you ask as part of interactive displays vary and challenge e.g.

* Some might be open, some closed.
* Some might be attention focusing.
* Some might encourage measurement or comparison.
* Some might provoke predictions or action.
* Some might pose problems.

Remember you will need to provide a means by which they can be answered – and the answers checked or else there is no purpose to them.

Making collections along a theme is an effective way of involving children as well as others to contribute and interact with a display. e.g. old things, treasures, patterns, hats etc. The contributors to the display should be encouraged to add information to the display about the objects they have brought.

The vocabulary used on displays should reinforce and extend that which has been introduced as part of a topic or a theme. The vocabulary list that follows suggests the type of language that might be included alongside art work  on display that has as its focus one or more of the elements or the language of Art and Design. The list is incomplete and it is intended that it should be added to and extended.

* **Line**
  Straight, curved, jagged, smooth, hard, soft, light, dark, thick, thin, long, short, broken, flowing, vertical, diagonal, horizontal, spiralling, angular, outline, broad, rhythmic, sweeping etc.

Can you work out what double 6 might be?
Think about the pattern in the answers!

Double 2 is...

Double 1 is...

*Make sure the types of questions you ask vary and are challenging.*

- **Tone**
  Light, dark, black, white, grey, shadow, highlight, contrast, shade.

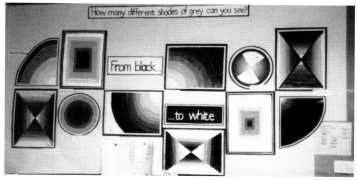

*Art and design labelling - Tone*

- **Colour**
  Warm, cold, light, dark, pale, deep, vibrant, dull, pastel, pure, bright, clashing, primary, secondary, shade, contrast.

*Colour*

- **Space**
  Open, enclosed, busy, large, small, confined, broad, high, wide, atmospheric, claustrophobic, airy, quiet, narrow.
- **Form**
  Cylinder, natural, man-made, sphere, cone, structure, volume, mass, weight, rigid, streamlined, cube, organic, malleable,

A discussion session when the children's answers to interactive displays are shared could be useful. It would give children the opportunity to clarify their answers if necessary, to give evidence to support and extend their answers, and to encourage the children to listen to and respond to each other's views and opinions. For the teacher this would also offer the opportunity to challenge the children's answers and to extend their thinking, understanding and interest in a display.

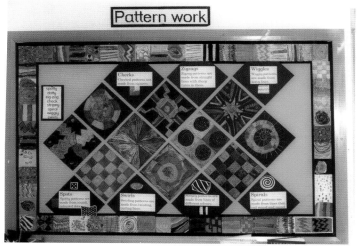

*Pattern*

- **Shape**
  Large, small, natural, man-made, geometric, solid, simple, complex, outline.
- **Texture**
  Rough, smooth, coarse, furry, glossy, feathery, hard, scratchy, slimy, waxy, silky, wet, dry, bubbly, woolly, bumpy, matt.
- **Pattern**
  Regular, rotating, repeat, irregular, symmetrical, border, natural, decorative, tessellating, grid, rhythm, half-drop.

*Texture*

Space for display in school is often inadequate or inappropriately sited – e.g. boards in Key Stage One are frequently fixed above the children's eye level. As space for all materials and resources are at a premium it is worth looking carefully at how the existing display areas are currently being used and consider their effectiveness and contribution to the learning environment. Some changes and suggestions as to alternative ways of displaying work may be necessary. Any changes will need discussion and consultation with all the staff involved as they may well have some good ideas and solutions to offer.

Points to Consider:

## Display Boards

*   Are there any walls/areas where additional display board could be put up for real effect e.g. over sinks?

*Labelling for organisation.*

*   Are any existing boards too narrow thus restricting the type of display that can be attempted and the amount of children's work that can go on display? Could these be put up elsewhere and replaced by wider ones?
*   Would it be useful to have some larger boards that extend from the floor upwards put in areas used by younger children so that there is scope for large friezes that they can touch and more work can be displayed at the children's eye level?
*   Are there wooden edges around some display boards which limit their use? If so could these boards be stripped of edging to make them

more versatile i.e. they could then be used for larger displays by extending the backing paper above, beyond and below the board.
*   Are there breeze block walls in school that are not being used for display? Work displayed on breeze block usually relies on Blu-tak to attach it and after several displays the wall often sports a residue of Blu-tak blobs which are unsightly and not always easy to remove. If display boards are not available a thin strip of wood along such a wall would allow backing paper with mounted work on it to be suspended from it securely as an additional display.

## Cupboards

*   Are there any cupboard fronts that could be boarded (especially old ones) to turn them into display areas?
*   Old cupboards can be given a new lease of life and their function easily identified if say the 'art club' paint appropriate motifs on them e.g. music notes and musical instruments on a music cupboard.

*Children's own labelling.*

*   Similarly old cupboards with their doors removed and insides painted can make attractive display areas for stimulus materials or 3D work. (See cover of this book.)
*   Old shoe lockers too with their doors removed and their insides painted can be used for display in the same way.

*Display boards above library shelves.*

*Good use made of a small display board.*

*Old cupboards given a new lease of life.*

*Using the corner of a room for an unmounted display on breeze blocks.*

- Both of the previous ideas are ideal for small immediate displays that are not easily disturbed but are readily altered and changed.

## Shelving

- Whereabouts are there areas of shelving e.g. corridors, resource areas, library etc?
- How attractive, useful or tidy are they? Who is responsible for them?
- Could any of this shelving be used more

*Shelving used for 3D display.*

effectively to display artefacts, stimulus materials, museum loan materials, 3D work etc?
- Displays here, if changed regularly, could become a focus and a learning resource for all.
- Could any additional shelving be installed for this purpose to make a storage area more attractive?
- Coloured paper on the wall behind the artefacts/ objects/ books on the shelves will make the display more eye-catching. Use the same colour of backing paper on display boards situated in the adjacent area for continuity and maximum impact.
- Shelves across a window alcove make a successful and protected area in which to display 3D work.
- Consider additional pinboard alongside or under these shelves for displays of tasks to be undertaken in the area or lists of monitors and their responsibilities regarding the area. Consider children's comments about the

artefacts on display or a quiz about the artefacts or work related to them.
- Old wooden bookshelves are ideal for displaying materials and resources on as well as books made by the class or individual children.

## Health and Safety Issues

- Note and make use of corridors, alcoves etc. for large impact work. Such areas are often narrow and badly lit. Would such an area benefit from additional lighting e.g. spotlights to highlight the displays so that they are more effective, viewed safely and treated with respect?

*3D display above a whiteboard.*

- Safety is an important factor to consider when siting or moving shelves, objects, display boards and pieces of work. Look carefully at the existing areas you are considering changing or the new area for display. Is there something you think could be dangerous? Is there anything that warns you of the danger? Is it likely an accident could happen? Consider the traffic in the area. Who might be at risk? How can you make it safer?
- Displaying work on the floor on boxes can be a danger and turn a corridor or entrance hall into an obstacle course.
- Work that protrudes from the wall if it is in a traffic area will likewise present problems and may be easily damaged.
- Work is often displayed in clip frames along corridor or traffic areas. The thinking behind this is that the work is protected, is made to look special and can easily be re-aligned if it is knocked. Make sure the clip frames in such areas are those that hold perspex over the

work and not glass which would be an added danger.

## Notice Boards

- Are there notice boards around school for both parents/visitors and children – are they obvious and easily viewed by their intended audience or are they badly placed and easily overlooked? Such notice boards often show pictures of the school staff or a plan of the school that indicates the position of various rooms.
- Is the information on them up to date? Does it keep readers informed of forthcoming events, clubs, meetings where to get the school uniform from etc.

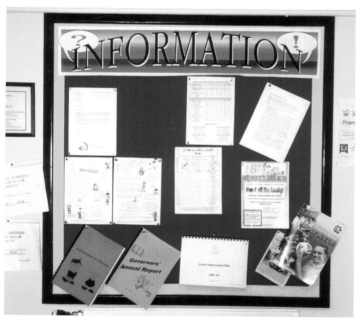

*Noticeboard for parents and visitors.*

- Are there notice boards for the staff (probably in the staff room) to keep them informed and up to date on current matters?
- Are there notice boards that inform individual children about their roles for the day or the week, or that give the children the result of sports fixtures, collections, house points, details of the school council etc.
- Is there a notice board for the children's own use?
- Notice boards need to be particularly well organised to be effective. Areas on them can easily be sectioned off with border roll or paper strips. Headings for each area should

be clearly printed. Sometimes blocks of colour used as backgrounds help to draw attention to a board or to divide it into different sections.

## Suspended Displays

Hanging objects from the ceiling is a useful display method. The possibilities for these will depend very much on the physical design of the school. Some buildings readily lend themselves to this whilst others clearly do not. Older buildings often have the advantage of exposed beams or piping which can be effectively utilised.

*A suspended display.*

Sensitive burglar alarm systems however have greatly limited this type of display. Safety is of extra importance here as it is necessary to avoid light fittings and to make sure everything is very secure and not likely to fall on the children's heads.

- P.E. hoops are light and easily suspended. Work can be hung both inside the hoops and suspended beneath them.
- Umbrella skeletons make good bases for mobiles e.g. for groups of related words.
- Wire coat hangers are easily collected and from them long threads of shapes can be suspended. It is a good idea to sellotape a join between the hook part of the coat hanger that loops over a line and the triangular shape of the hanger itself so that it is not as easily dislodged.
- Many classrooms now sport washing lines or webs of nylon thread across the room attached to wall hooks at adult head height -

quite hazardous to a visiting adult! It is easy to clutter and fill all the hanging space now on offer and to end up with an untidy, distracting and disjointed display. Arrange the work in an organised way i.e. in rows, groups or blocks with gaps and breathing spaces between each group. This way it will be easier to identify and use the work e.g. 'colour words' and also to appreciate the children's contributions.

## Going Under

Changing areas of the school into a display environment is a rich educational experience and one that offers a different approach to display.

*Display under window ledges.*

- e.g. create a jungle environment by painting plants on the windows, suspending fronds, leaves, flowers and butterflies from the ceiling and add some large scale 3D plants and tape recordings of bird, insect and animal sounds. This will offer a display for the children to sit in, wander through etc.
- Use rolls of corrugated paper to make a cave for the children to go in and add their own cave paintings.
- Use a clothes maiden to create a tent with eastern style artefacts etc. All of these offer a different type of interactive display.

*3D Display on a free standing screen.*

## Screens - Hide it and Tidy it

- Screens are a versatile display resource within a school. They allow bays to be created, areas to be changed and divided and can be used either singly or in groups. They vary considerably in weight, quality and height and it is worth looking carefully at a range of different types available if new ones are to be purchased. Screens that are too lightweight can be a danger as they may overbalance but on the other hand those that are too heavy and cumbersome may deter people from using them. It is also necessary to consider where they are going to be stored when they are not in use. The surface of the screens should be neutral and able to take a number of different fixings e.g. velcro, straight pins etc.

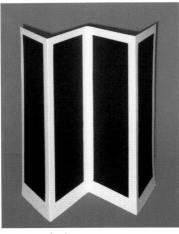

*A zig zag screen.*

42

- Large card concertina (zig-zag) books can be stood under table tops to create further display areas. They will also hide and disguise bulky resources and those that are used less frequently.
- Rolls of corrugated paper can also be used as screens. They tend to be rather unstable and are best unfurled to make a series of bays with a chair behind each bay for support. Pinning work on to corrugated paper is not an easy task – be warned!
- Curtains around a table will disguise and make what is kept under it less distracting. Likewise, less frequently used resources can be kept out of sight when not in use behind a screened off corner of the classroom.
- Mess and general untidiness around under or next to any display will detract from the impact of the display itself. Take a look – tidy it up – it will be well worth it in the long run. More suggestions follow in the section on storage.

## Windows

In many new buildings display space is limited because of large expanses of windows which present quite a challenge as a display area. It is difficult to attach work successfully to glass for a length of time no matter what type of fixings are used e.g. glue, sellotape, Blu-tak etc. Many of these will provide only temporary adhesion and will fail if (a) the work is too heavy or (b) if the schools suffers with condensation and (c) the room is very sunny. Sellotape often leaves unsightly marks on the glass that are not easy to remove.

- Remember that displays on windows are seen from the outside as well as from within and it is worth considering the impression the display will give from this angle when arranging the work.
- If the windows have wooden frames work can be attached to them by Blu-tak or by clipping work in bulldog type clips that hang from the window frame on lengths of string.
- Garden netting across a window will also provide a surface to which work can be clipped.
- It is important to consider the 'light' factor when using window space for display. An

*A blocked up window used as a display alcove.*

*Shelves allow 3D display to be seen from inside and outside.*

over-enthusiastic display could plunge a room into darkness!

- An effective use of windows for display is to paint on them. There are many brands of paint suitable for this purpose. This special paint is designed to be translucent i.e. to let the light through, not to dry out and crack and flake, to resist condensation and not to run, and to be easily cleaned off. Children can easily be the makers of such displays as the windows will hopefully be within their reach. For some topics e.g. an underwater scene, painted on a window will considerably add to and stimulate the environment.

*Many brands of paint are suitable for painting on glass.*

## Working Areas

Many classroom are set out so that each part of the room is used for a specific purpose e.g. book corner, role play area, maths area, art area etc. and the appropriate resources are kept there to be used. Much will depend, of course, on the space available within the room.

- Setting out working areas needs careful consideration – to avoid congestion and to provide quiet areas e.g. book corners away from where more active learning is explored.
- The positioning of furniture in order that the children can easily be seen and have easy access to each area is of course a health and safety issue. An initial arrangement may need several modifications before it functions smoothly and safely.
- Consideration will need to be given to display the range of tools and resources to be used, the tasks to be undertaken, and the number of children to use the area at one time etc.
- Displays in each area should include lists, labels and charts etc. related to its particular function. If attractively arranged and set out, this can make a considerable contribution to the overall appearance of the classroom.
- For example a writing area might include:
  Tables and chairs.
  Notices, timetables, labels and charts.
  Messages about the current day.
  Child written and child dictated work
  Directions about activities.
  Varied supplies of pens, pencils, paper etc.
  Books, magazines, newspapers etc.

*A well laid out
Writing Corner.*

*An interesting Role Play Area.*

*An easily accessible Book Corner.*

*A well equipped Art Area.*

# Storing Materials, Equipment and Resources

Each subject area has and needs its own range of materials, equipment and resources. It is always difficult to know how and where it is best to store these so that they are readily available and easily accessible to both staff and children. They need to be kept tidy, well organised and cared for, so that they are not wasted or damaged.

Some items will need to be kept in individual classrooms for day to day use, others may be kept in a resource or library area whilst some bulky items need to be stored in the general stock cupboard.

A wide range of storage containers, boxes, trays, tubs etc. are available in most educational supplier's catalogues. Before buying any containers, make yourself familiar with what is already in school. This will make matching and adding to the existing storage facilities much easier and economical.

DIY stores now offer a range of reasonably priced storage crates in a variety of sizes and colours. Also many containers can be collected by the children themselves as the packaging today in which many goods are delivered make ideal storage containers e.g. plastic sweet jars.

*Uniform storage for easy recognition*

## In the Classroom

- First look carefully at what is already in place. Is it adequate and appropriate or are the containers too full, too old and no longer suitable?
- Do the children take responsibility for keeping the storage tidy and if necessary replenished? If not why not? Perhaps it is inappropriately placed and access is difficult.
- To improve the appearance of the room colour co-ordinate storage boxes for uniformity. Whether they are **on** a surface or **under** a surface if they are all the **same colou**r it will give a sense of unity to the room. You may need to exchange containers with other members of staff to get enough of the colour range you want- believe me co-ordinated colour will make a difference and can tidy up a range of resources that previously looked a mess. Regard the storage and presentation of materials as part of the display within a room.

*Colour coordinated storage containers.*

- Also look for, order or purchase containers that are **similar in shape and size** and that will group together easily in rows or blocks. This type of related arrangement will again add to the organised appearance of a room.

- Files and folders that are of a similar colour and trays and tubs that match will also give a sense of unity.
- Make sure all resources are clearly labelled and that the lettering used on each is consistant. Messy, mis-matched and untidy labels are distracting and can spoil the effect of a well mounted display on the wall above them.
- Look at how the storage containers are used by the children. If they are well placed but not in the way, children can be encouraged to be responsible for returning tools and resources to their appropriate place after they have finished using them thus helping to keep the classroom tidy.

*Files and folders of a similar colour.*

- Trays and containers for finished work or work to be given out need to be considered to avoid untidy and messy piles of books on every surface.
- Containers for scissors, pencils, rulers etc. for the middle of each table need to be stable and again if possible uniform.
- An important consideration for any area of storage, whether in the classroom or outside it which is being used by the children independently, is – Do the children know where things belong? - if they don't things will get into a mess and a muddle very quickly.

## In the Resource Area

This is an area that will be used by several classes and probably for a range of different purposes.

- The materials and equipment in this area will be easier to find if the area is divided up into different sections – each section storing materials for a different curriculum area. To make it easier each section could be colour co-ordinated. If this is not possible then use a range of containers that are similar in shape and size.
- All storage containers here will again need to be clearly labelled and, if they are to be accessed by the children, arranged at an appropriate height.
- Shelves too need labels so that materials and equipment can be returned to their rightful place after they have been used.

*Using sweet jars for storage.*

- This is an area where it is likely that teacher resources i.e. pictures and stimulus material will also be kept. Transparent wallets are ideal for pictures. These could be labelled by topic, artist etc. Objects used for stimulus could be stored on shelves or in open cupboards.

*Clearly labelled teacher's resources.*

- As the materials and equipment stored in this area are likely to be borrowed by a number of classes it is a good idea to devise a system of tracking them down if they are needed. One method is to give each class a series of labels each with the class name on it. When an item is borrowed one of these labels is put in its place on the shelf until the item is returned.

- Equipment is often stored in class cupboards and forgotten about rather than in resource areas where it could be better used. It is a good idea to have a session when the staff all bring equipment out of their cupboards and decisions are made as to its future storage. This can also help avoid duplicating, by error, equipment that was already plentiful and in school.

*Clear labelling helps children to be responsible for the classroom environment.*

# The Stock Cupboard

This cupboard is usually every Art Co-ordinator's nightmare as it never seems to stay tidy and stock runs out before they are notified and have a chance to order more. Storage, organisation, labelling and accessibility are paramount if stock is to be found readily, used appropriately, remain undamaged and returned when surplus to requirements. It is often small in space with a number of small narrow shelves and little area for successful paper storage.

*A "five star" stock cupboard.*

- Look at the way it is being used and abused at present before making any major alterations and get to know what stock there already is, what is useful, what is past its sell by date and what is lacking. Sometimes stock orders remain the same year after year and materials pile up that are unwanted, unnecessary and take up valuable space.

- Decide on storage that is adequate and storage that is needed both in terms of boxes, shelves etc.

- The stock for Art and Design would be easier to find if it were arranged according to the technique it is designed to serve i.e. drawing, painting, printing, collage, textiles and 3D. There will of course be some overlap e.g. between collage and textiles. If each area was colour co-ordinated, it would make finding and returning stock an easy procedure.

- Decisions will also need to be taken as to how the stock is displayed and arranged in the cupboard i.e. the items that are light and easy to lift and that can go on the higher shelves, the bulky items and boxes that might be better lower down and the heavy items and paper that needs to go on the floor or in a paper store under the shelves.

- If there is space this is a useful area in which to keep large paper cutters particularly if there is also a clear working top on which they can be used.

*Effective paper storage*

50

- The display kit (see page 7) could also be kept in here together with any useful Art and Design books for the staff.
- Paper is often a difficult material to store and move about. It is better if it can be divided into colours – ideally in two paper stores, one for black, white, grey, cream and brown and the other for coloured paper. If the paper can be arranged in small separated piles of each colour it will

*An effective way of storing posters or big books.*

be easier to move around and less likely to get damaged.
- Tissue paper needs to be stored in a closed cupboard away from the light so that it does not fade.
- Paper is often ordered in large sizes only and much time is then spent in cutting it into smaller pieces. Storing large sheets of paper is also difficult if the shelves are narrow. It soon becomes creased and torn along the edges. Most educational suppliers will cut or provide paper in smaller sizes and it might be worth considering ordering some paper in future that is already cut to both A3 and A4 size.

- Poster paper is very popular as display paper but two of its bright colours together can be a bit overpowering. It does however work well as a background for some of the more subdued shades of sugar paper that may have piled up in the corner of the stock cupboard and are seldom used. This is well worth a mention.
- It is a good idea to have an exercise book in the cupboard in which staff can list items they feel are lacking and those they would like for a future project.
- A list of the different items stored in the stock cupboard would be useful for each member of staff to have – plus one on the back of the stock cupboard door.
- Regular checks will be needed to ensure that items of stock do not run out long before the next stock order is due. I have never found that leaving a book in the stock cupboard for this purpose is effective.
- Some stock e.g. glue sticks, cartridge paper etc. is often misused and it might be worthwhile to discuss the match of materials to task at a staff meeting in order that extravagance for convenience sake does not take over.
- A wise Art co-ordinator doesn't put all the new stock out at once but saves some of it in another cupboard for later in the year and to encourage the staff to use up the old stock first.

# Display Outside the Classroom

There are many areas within school that are also used for display purposes. It is essential to inform staff for which of these areas they are responsible beyond their own classroom as it is daunting to suddenly find out that the only blank piece of wall in school is yours and no-one has told you about it. It is also a good idea to stipulate a deadline for when displays in these areas must be up.

Working to a deadline does not always ensure that displays appear on time – but it helps!   It is also useful to have a realistic timescale as to how often during the course of the term these displays are expected to be changed – or else they can become very faded, out of date and tatty.

## Corridors

These are often busy traffic areas so work on display here needs to be carefully planned and securely attached to the board.

If there are a series of adjacent boards down a corridor it is advisable to link them by colour i.e. using the same colour backing paper on each one even if the work  itself on each board is not related. This will have more impact and  the overall effect will be more pleasing, than if each board is a different colour.

Work displayed in corridors is sometimes linked by means of a collaborative theme e.g. Change, Stories etc. Suggestions for display themes are to be found towards the end of the book.

Whatever the work, it needs to be labelled carefully with the name of the class or the year group involved so that the children still have ownership of it even if it is away from their room.

Corridors are ideal areas for recycling and sharing work that has been done in the classroom and viewed only by those children involved.  Such displays will lessen the workload on the staff who only need to move and reposition the work. This will give status and added value to the work that has been produced by their class. It also informs children and visitors of  the type of work being undertaken by the different age groups.

Corridors make good 'Galleries' if inexpensive picture frames are purchased. Work mounted in such frames can be displayed safely, is easy to reposition if dislodged and is not easily damaged. It is also easy to change the work on display. Poetry and stories as well as art work can be displayed in the 'Gallery'. As an additional touch, display a photograph of the (child) author or artist next to the work and ask him/her to write

*A long corridor display reflecting work on India.*

*A corridor display based on children's novels.*

*A corridor display depicting class portraits.*

Another approach is to record on tape the children talking about their work and to display a tape recorder near the work together with an invitation to the onlooker to listen to these comments that accompany it.

Displays that protrude into corridors whether at eye level or on the floor can be a Health and Safety hazard unless these features are a permanent fixture that the children have always encountered and are used to avoiding.

a little about themselves and their work to accompany the frame.

# The Entrance

The entrance in any school is an important display area as this is where visitors get their first impression of the school. It is an area that needs to be kept tidy, and interesting at all times. Entrance areas benefit from notices to inform the visitor where to go to seek help, to find a particular room etc. The lettering on such notices needs to be consistent, and notices need to be sited where they are obvious, but not intrusive, and are easy to read.

It is often an area that is appropriate for a parent's notice board detailing forthcoming events, meetings etc. Some schools use this area as a 'Gallery', displaying framed children's work and a collection of books and interesting objects. Other schools provide information in this area about the school uniform, the school brochure and pictures of the current members of staff.

Schools that have had an artist in residence working with the children often use this area to display a permanent piece of work that has been created during the artist's time in school together with photographs of the children involved in its making. A collection of indoor plants will enhance any display providing they are are in good condition and not dead or dying!

Whatever the display, make sure it is welcoming and gives the right message about the work of the school and its values – remember first impressions count.

*A permanent display in an entrance hall.*

*An entrance hall "bursting with children's work".*

*A large notice board in a school hall.*

# The Hall

This is often a difficult area in which to display work as it is continually in use and has many different functions throughout the day. It is not an area for fragile displays if it is used for P.E. or even for permanent displays if class assemblies require their own individual back drops. This is an area where display screens can be useful as displays on them can easily be moved and repositioned. Some halls have large display boards in them, others have none. If the walls are being used for display it is nice if each class or Key Stage can make a contribution – after all it is used by all. Sometimes e.g. at Christmas it is a good idea to have a colour scheme that is used in all the work on display for continuity and to link the different boards together. On other occasions the displays may have a specific theme (e.g. Ourselves) that is

*A grid arrangement of Key Stage 1 work.*

approached in a different way by each of the classes. As many halls, particularly in old schools, have high ceilings the space lends itself to large pieces of collaborative work, e.g. banners and hangings, to provide a display with impact and in some cases semi-permanence. The hall is an area that readily lends itself to exhibitions of work that focus on a particular area of the curriculum e.g. Design and Technology. When it is being used for this purpose, screens, tables, drama blocks etc. will all come into use. Many of these will need to be covered in order to link them, disguise them and to focus on the work on display. Use plain coverings and consider carefully the colours that are used next to each other and on the screens or walls behind the work. Link a screen/board and the table /boxes below it by colour. Make sure the traffic areas around the exhibition are easy to access and that all labels are firmly attached to items on display and the display itself – it is easy for them to disappear and go walkabout leaving the viewer puzzled as to what the work has really been about!

*Wall hangings used in a hall with many doors and high ceilings.*

## Outside the Building

It is worth looking carefully at the outside of the building particularly the areas where the children enter and leave it and where they play. Would a painted display on the outside walls enhance and improve the overall appearance of the building – or would it be a target for graffiti and vandalism?

Some schools have involved the children in the planning and drawing of designs for such displays which have later been executed by an adult – often an artist in residence. In this way children share ownership of their outdoor environment, know that their ideas are valued and enjoy and appreciate seeing them materialise. Outdoor storage for toys and equipment is often a shed or a lorry back, which, with a bit of imagination and a lick of paint, can become items of interest in the environment.

*Outside storage for toys painted as a fire engine.*

Enclosed garden or glass sided courtyard areas, which are relatively vandal free, provide ideal sites for pieces of sculpture that can constantly be seen and enjoyed from within the school building. Garden areas (flowerbeds in particular) require constant upkeep and attention if they are to contribute a good display. An overgrown and neglected garden area soon fills with litter and rubbish and can then detract from rather than enhance the school environment.

Colourful displays of flowers and plants that are changed as the seasons change can become a focal point to be enjoyed and appreciated as well as a rich source for learning. Children can be involved in the care and upkeep of such gardens as their contribution to improving the school environment. Schools where garden areas are likely to be vandalised have found that container displays which are taken in at night is one way to overcome this problem without losing the benefit of live, growing and colourful displays of plants.

*Children helped plan and draw this design.*

*Painted walls can enhance the appearance of a drab school building.*

# What to Avoid and Why

There are no hard and fast rules that will ensure a good display, as, hopefully this book has shown. It does however offer suggestions that if considered can help in the selection of colours, mounting and arrangement of work all of which contribute to the success of a display. As teachers we are all individuals with our own individual styles and approaches to the same task and which is to be encouraged. However some of us have more confidence than others! What follows is a prompt sheet, a list of things to consider when embarking on a display which hopefully will help avoid pitfalls and make the task of displaying work less of a burden when time is precious.

## DO

- Aim for initial planning of the layout before starting - see how the individual pieces of work fit together best to form a united group.

- Aim for simplicity rather than over crowding – too much work can crowd, clutter and detract from the impact of a display.

- Co-ordinate and carefully consider the choice of colours to be used – if the mounts and the background colours don't work well together the display will be less effective.

- Reflect colours that are in the children's work – particularly if it is art work as this will emphasise and support the work on display.

- Include questions – to encourage the children to investigate and use the display.  Also consider how they are going to record the answers to these questions.

- Make sure the lettering and labelling is clear, of a high standard and appropriately placed - to provide a role model for the children and to make sure the information about the display can be read.

- Use appropriate vocabulary – this will reinforce and share the new vocabulary that has been introduced whilst the work on display was in progress.

- Aim for continuity of colour throughout the classroom or adjoining areas – too many colours on adjacent display boards can be overpowering and detract from the different displays.

- Explain the reasons/ process and show the progression of the work undertaken within the display – this will explain to the viewer how the finished pieces of work were achieved and what was learnt. It also gives scope to display the work from a larger number of children.

- Mix dimensions i.e. include 3D and 2D examples - this will enrich a display and show that different and individual responses to the same starting point have been considered and encouraged.

*A mixture of 2D and 3D work creates an interesting contrast.*

- Display stimulus material alongside the children's work- this will show what the children have used, looked at and discussed as a starting point for their work.

- Have a recognisable theme / title – work on untitled displays is not as readily understood or appreciated as when the title provides the necessary information.

- Mount the work uniformly – use the same colours for each piece of work even if the mount widths vary according to the size of the different pieces.

- Have a focal point and an apt focus title – this will grab attention and invite the onlooker to further investigate a display. It may be larger or mounted differently from the rest of the lettering / work on the display.

- Aim for well balanced arrangements with regular spaces between pieces of work – this will make the display more pleasing and easy on the eye.

*Stimulus material alongside childrens' work.*

- Make sure reading matter is displayed at children's eye level – this is not easy as space is limited but ideally we want the children who view the display to investigate and find out what it is about.

- Make sure every child has work on display at some time – this is vital to build children's confidence and to show each child that their contribution is necessary and valued.

- Display a variety of work so that displays have cross-curricular links between different subject areas e.g. art and history can provide visually stimulating displays.

- Tidy the area under and adjacent to displays – untidy areas detract from the work displayed on the wall.

- Remember all displays should be free from sharp edges, corners and surfaces- Health and Safety issues are paramount. No one should be able to be injured by a display e.g. cut fingers.

*Stimulus material can enhances the end product.*

# DON'T

- Don't cut irregular bubbles around children's work – as soon as a piece of work is cut round and changes shape the quality of the work is in danger of being destroyed. It becomes different rather than improved. However it is different if on occasion unusual shaped pieces of paper have been provided for the work as then they become a necessary and integral part of design.

- Don't cut around children's work using pinking shears - ragged edges will not improve the appearance of the work unless this type of cutting relates to the theme e.g. frost.

- Use brass headed drawing pins – in large numbers these glint and wink and distract from the work!

- Mount and arrange pictures at a slant both on a background mount or on the wall itself. Art galleries hang pictures in rows so that they are easily viewed and appreciated, not at a slant so that the viewer has to tilt his/her head to view the work from a variety of angles. Slanted work is distracting and puzzling to the eye.

- Avoid overcrowding – too much and the impact of the work is lost rather than appreciated as the eye is unsure where to look first and how to make sense of the display.

- Make sure there is sufficient contrast between the mounting and the backing paper - too much contrast and the work gets lost in a riot of colour, too little contrast and the display is dull and ineffective.

- Avoid fussy, unnecessary drapes and borders- keep it simple. If a display is too busy, the work and information becomes lost among a wealth of added extras.

- Don't put hand written lettering too high or make it too thick - it detracts and can look messy, particularly if it is uneven and badly spaced. Also the aim is that it should be easily and comfortably read. Remember - check your spelling!

- Don't make cut out letters so fancy that they become difficult to read – they may look attractive but they have been put there to inform and be read rather than just to decorate.

- Don't choose and use a computer font for labels that is similarly difficult to read - check with the children that they can read and have read the captions, questions and labels on the display. If the font is too "arty" the chances are that they will be ignored.

- Don't simply dot pictures about with irregular gaps between them - a planned, simple straight forward orderly arrangement will be more pleasing and have greater impact.

- Don't have single mounts too thin - work mounted this way will lack strength and look lost on a large board.

- Don't have frieze backgrounds pale and 'wishy washy' - strong colour is best for impact where large pieces of work are concerned.

- Don't label untidily, haphazardly or indistinctly. The display will lack focus, appear muddled and be difficult to follow and understand.

- Don't leave out labels- the viewer may be rather puzzled or the display ignored.

- Don't put labels where they can't be read by the target audience i.e. too high or too low –
e.g. if they are for adults rather than children the height will need to be adjusted accordingly.

- Don't only display commercial products - these make quick, immediate displays and are ideal to start a topic but only before there is material contributed by the children.

- Don't put unconnected random work/ items together - link the materials on display in a sequence or group them in a way that is logical and easily understood.

- Don't obscure work by overlapping it too extremely- a display arranged this way will appear overloaded and cluttered.

- Don't do every display in the same way / type of layout – much will depend on the content of the display but try to go for a variety of approaches in the course of a term or year to awake and stimulate the children's interest in their learning environment.

Ignoring these rules and suggestions can however on occasion result in stunning displays! Display is not a subject area where any one approach will guarantee the ideal outcome each time.

# Themes for Collaborative and Seasonal Displays

Some of these themes may be more appropriate to Key Stage One, others to Key Stage Two whilst some are appropriate to both Key Stages and would be suitable for whole school displays when each year group is responsible for a separate board as part of the display. Examples include:

- Numbers, Shapes, Measures, Letters, Stories, Poems, Sound, Light.

- Materials, Changes, Seasons, Weather, Clothes, Homes, Cooking.

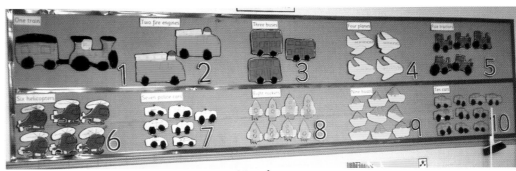

*Numbers*

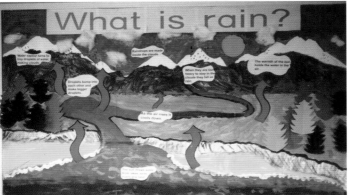

*Weather*

*Poems: The Jabberwocky*

- Gardening, Transport, People, Families and Friends, Time, Animals.

- Cause and Effect, Plants, Growing, Toys, Old and New, Up and Down.

- Clothes, Hats, Books, Machines, Holes and Cavities, Spaces, Buildings.

- Festivals and Celebrations, Contrasts (Day / Night, Happy / Sad).

- Qualities (Shining, Reflecting), Colour, Pattern, Texture, Lines, Minibeasts.

*Plants*

- Machines, North American Indians, Sea, Dreams, Inside / Outside, Future worlds.

- Space, Rocks, Nests, Underground, Destruction, Myths, Chaos.

- Harmony, Gates and Fences, Distortion, Flight, Circus, Games, Sport.

- Energy, Magic, A School Visit, Wood, Jewellery, Dragons, Events, Discoveries.

- Large and Small, Pollution, Shells, Movement, The Senses, Memorabilia.

- Jungles, Services, Windows and Doors, Kings and Queens, Races.

- Fables, Masquerade, Spirals, Nets, Networks, Fire and Water, Printing.

- Islands, Castles, Constructions, Contrasts, Surfaces, Markets, Religions.

- Deserts, Camouflage, Music, Puppets, Wrappers, Splash, Bubbles.

- Mystery, Treasure, Communication, Surprises, Unexpected Happenings,

- In a Garden, What is it Made Of? Holidays, Masks and Drums, Help, etc. etc!!

Some of these themes link naturally to specific areas of the curriculum, e.g. science, whilst others are cross-curricular and could be interpreted through a range of different subject areas.

*Aboriginal Art*

*Masks and Drums*

*Science*

*Sport*

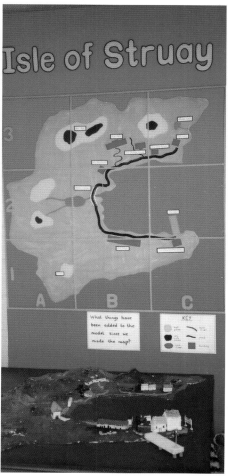

*Geography*

*Jungle*

*History*